GHOST SONGS

Ghost Songs

POEMS

William Pettit

Casagrande Press • San Diego

Published by Casagrande Press
San Diego, California

www.casagrandepress.com
casagrandepress@aol.com

All work copyright © 2002, 2009 William Pettit

All rights reserved. No part of this publication may be reproduced or transmitted in any form or by any means, electronic or mechanical, including photocopy, recording, or any information storage and retrieval systems, without prior written permission from the publisher, except for reviewers who wish to quote brief passages.

Front cover art: "Untitled" by William Pettit
Book Design: Steve Connell / Transgraphic Services

Printed in the USA

Every phrase and every sentence is an end and a beginning,
Every poem an epitaph.

—T. S. Eliot

Ghost Songs 11

Canti Isolani 43

SchoolGirlSongs 51

Birthday Suites 67

The SomeHighway Poems 81

Ghost Songs

A Landscape

The hemmed work of the half moon tonight
On the horizon
Launching flags and shuttles of smoke but still
Still
As a wolf-prairie;
What is not bleached by the dim fallen clouds
is absorbed in its own depth, and turned black

still are the blue pines above the ghosts.

Color Study

The mountains are blue, the fields pink to gold
the sky full of soft chickens
Darkness is only one, heavy and empty, warm and cool together.
The town is yellow, your house is heavy
rosewhite in the morning, steel grey the afternoon
when your window recovers from its highlight, and
the roof begins to blush
then bleed, then rust, then turn completely back   to night
one fifth a fists worth of yellow light

The sound hurt, the light went out

Nomentana

Before the summer of departure
I lived in an old people's hole under the Squirrel Hill highway

poverty in the Pittsburgh winter.

at a fashionable alternative concert or
perhaps somewhere in the halls of the Italian department
I saw her

then it was Easter.
I brought a sugary present shaped like a bunny
For dinner
There was expensive wine, it was Hairy
as an Italian

At Nomentana station now all trams and trains
Once an address in Brazil, once a long distance call,
Now across town on my hands and feet.

Salt Is the Salt of Life

Watching the TV floods and drinking the *Torri*'d wine
The Queen's hem and the war,
Salt is the salt of life, I said
On bended wing and wounded knee
Like blood to the steak and steak to the bone

All the bridges in the rain over the foaming Po
Like over Panther Hollow to the Spanish Frick
Or the guano canal, from Queens, with NY lit, to Greenpoint
      my Brooklyn barracks.
And on the Ides of October marching
Ponte Milvio, from Rome, over the rapid Tiber, to Rome
      The moon as big as the city and filthy yellow
      behind the torches of Corso Francia,
      its arch made circle on the still side
And walked the Manhattan Bridge, in a scattered group, moving from
      Discomfort to Drunkenness
      that Chinese Apocalypse in the cold spring
And over the Brooklyn Bridge with an Italian, seeing the mosque of
      money, and Philip Glass between the twin towers
      when, itchy after work, I wanted to buy a t-shirt
      but instead stopped
at Border's.

The overgrown Po is the Lega's fault
Getting wet is mine.

The Flag of The Neverlands

A short circuit from broken bark, my fire of wisteria and wet leaves
All fallen feathers of the stark season
From the fog and smoke of engines the steel glitters, cold   until
    above them we pass

I chucked the stump with a paddle, the axe handle hit dryly to thy
    wrist then elbow then o shoulder

& with the same hand slowly paint
The Flag of the Neverlands

While the continents shift.

After a Storm

All the town-yellows are equal   after,
heavy caravans   move like continents,
the clouds push
northward where no shadows were
now vacant

everything just grew

★   ★   ★

chiselled under the slate
  where homes are
the clear   just before night.

You may have   two colors : One   for every element
the cliffside counts as earth;
    the mountain is sky

★   ★   ★

now gone
the grey volcano
the blue is cloud and white   the sky

a horizon

doesn't relate.

Forget about how your   house looks.

False Autumn

A wash, a line of smoke
There that fire, that hill   the farmers bundle around
Under the olives and the foil

Heavy blue edges go under
from chimney to tombstone

and lets loose smoke like a foghorn stops
          then flames back in red
it indicates itself   with white
windward disappearing
where birds do.

Field Work

Dotted glass soldiers form the horizon
gather in the glow of pitchforks—
heads driven down
        of rivets, the sharp edge.

Any formation is a mob.
I deem the burrows
the sullen mailbag squat, with you

By the ends of me let the dead fall to their own
By our own hands let's be cast into the sand

And to think it was the last winter to fear—
"I've spoken now and forever   "

To don the miracle or no
To spot the coming blue jay,
hawk late winters exhaust
from Umbria
from the North.

March   *to a battered thumb*

As long as my long arms grow
Finding deep bitter   & sanding off the cut's splinter,
My thumb
On the sides of grounded weeds, patched over with seed
The split-hoe coughing rocks

As long as the fire takes the moss & the *malva*
out

An arm on every rock, my militant throw
To help out the hungry cat   & the shades of his want
To lick first the T-bone and the stick
Before   dogwards   letting go.

Wandering out through the curtain, after midnight,
into the moon's hole
the backwards head of a blackbird
To my group of stars   said

Hunt me
With ne' slingshot nor rake.

March Waltz

Hand in the bully
to you,
Fragrant palms.
This is the butter that moves you.

Year-wise, we gave up
the plan .
Dried pumpkins ticked like clocks

      Mud made the pigs' blanket until the rain called it off

We took our Shells
down the slopes of the ravine
Where foxholes made a city
& calcium-cicles drool like dry-ice-smoke
under roots

I aim the slingshot

See that fire, that ghost?

March Yet

Looking long at your frankenstein arms, the sleeves that cover
The side the whole mountain'd face—
The birds cry from being in my pan
Alternate from bent to jointed
& undo it again

It's March if the cherry-sparrows carpet the budding
Where   I buried the seeds   shallow
    in afterthought
when deep tulips and I   lift big stones and small stones.

Sheepshit and straw shipwreck in a whirlpool
That I build pyramids above the roots with
and simulate erosion with hose and boots

        Someone sinks a fence post / notches on a scale
        Popcorns off the house and over the valley
        Shrapnel accelerates and stops.

The only thing vital to mystery is ignorance.

Morning Motion

Scared for the flora in this emptiness.

Drain the pollen bags
Under my eyes / run water
Dull steps towards the dusty afternoon
Drops, compresses, steam

The coffee   the morning   is mighty
extract dripping more
concentration, while the sunshine tells lies, haze varies   temper
        & swelling attests to pressure.
The wind relieves the winter and rattles the grass.

Spring   is sworn in
on its own   four   calf-wobbling feet
It's not the rain but the waiting.

Hurray for the brushfire, hurray for the haze
Who turn the land   blank

Hurray, like the sky.

Sketch from a Live Model

Sandbags is my bladder
Heaving sides, a bucket.

Where eyes and ears confront
the universe, tender pores bruised.

My witness weighs and aches
are hooks in my face,   trans-
parent tar, to brittle my tubes.

Batters and clicks, as if a bird
fluttering punctured, my pump
only a vampire could restore.

There are some charred trunks, unsettled scabs
those aiming, and those resigning to lump. Then
elegant silver pencil marks, an alphabet, the scars.

What's my side to you I have no idea, in the blind
field of the blankets, in summertime/mirrored well
and turning thinner/ salt bleach cleaned

What's pink reddens, white (at least) ochres,
maybe roses.

Someone Else's Lament & Prayer (with a sawed-off shotgun)

I can stand the missing crown
Broken weather, dust.
With some thought, I can figure the distance
& either stock up, or sleep.

To fill the bucket   I adjust
    Just sit out the storm &
stay warm.

Even where the river was
Is dry   all year.

       Writing   for "the   general   good"
       In jotted landscapes
       In the season of the white sky
               —shades of violet above the haze
       Faint   with heavy hand—

I can bear the brunt of "the cruellest month" & stand the swarms
I see why sometimes it's so loud
                                then dead.

Makes you want to shoot every sign.

Swordsworth

The filter quiets the turnpike

off the road is black   from the headlights

straight workhorse/ blind burrow
in windows of coal
snow banks & hawks

pay the gates to the hilly outskirts, the dark drive
all lanes, then all lit houses, constellation
on the glass: coffee steam
mountain gas

every morning is cold & Virginia-misty

Sixteen wheels on the Keller's fields
one blue Amish summer

down Panther Hollow, all stairs

★   ★   ★

The rain comes endless today
dissolves to smoke
Fields and their dark trees, senseless,
today dissolve and wither into it.

Thigh Mt.

There is snow atop this morning the mountain
Late-season-snow, from hip to knee
From the blue triangle up, yanked-white-weather
mutes the bed.
North goes the hip, waist where the Flaminia lies—low road with
      lumps
To pale Reatine bosom
Blushed by winds further up, with a little sugar.

      Smoke disconnects from a circle of cypress
The land-fire becomes clouds

Arms rest along the river, fingers of delta
On the shoulders, umber-shadowed back
      abandoned under the moon   and   fields forever

Pinks rust in the dark
You are
another mountain somewhere

In it, a lake.

Three-Nap-Day *for a cracked thumb-bone*

> *On bummed knee*
> *Trying to qualify why*
> *The bruised bone is always Left:*
> *Thumb or fractured index.*

Today the fault goes to a fascist hammer, the back side of an axe
Once before split the same thumb open
Cuticle toned   Tabernacle
Choirs go   from nail to neck.

The rawhide   tomorrow   will help
While dressed up for hoeing
      When I'll recall a dark Pgh street towards the Northside, then the
        airport, then suddenly above
      The cathedral, & Soldiers & Sailors
        and dream Orte, a cavern *sotto* Orvieto, a red spider & my bèby—-
I'll wait for the gloves to crust and
The sun
      to boil out the fat off my back.

The other limp is in the temple, and due to dust: what
All living things do   in spring

The X-ray of my left hand
Holding
And the long line up
from the nail on

and a host of other things

Green Force Map

                Force becometh
                Joyce, the one
                Who'd sand me

                        Did I leaveyouforsomething good—

Among shell bones, married couples
and unanimous reservations

Begotten by fog
One to the other
Offered oysters
One sterling morning
With the huffy subaru
Raw flesh gift
To cook with
      Menemsha

★   ★   ★

Hurdled above by loose stars firing
The long last summer now crescent
the season of masks
The beaches cold   at no cost
We
with visor-hidden lists
Gave sense   —ridded us of us,
not taking pain away

        the past I understand / From the title of a book
          at the Library   our Bikes
how did we always have nothing else to do?

MVY, many apt paths and
seasides—
Don't consider me among the mighty, not here.

★   ★   ★

If you can afford me crosswise
In a blind handshake   of tangled hair:

I'll give you what you steal
If I can keep what I rob
Deal?

don't call the kettle black unless your cattle can handle the dirtywork

Will it begin, the wind to whistle
Under now born almond flowers
I fear the frost.

Will it   wind

     I owe a great deal to birth
     They fit me   with the latest

     Now it's too late   to cancel me
         an ample cheese sandwich is in my ham
     The bread laws,   Fixd

     No need to battle with the wheat

if the bucks don't shelve it, I will.

Poem On Leaving

The rain tonight came senseless.
I thought of lining the gates
I thought of emptying out.

The sky was like a well-tossed sea
Heavy   & opened up
light came
& hollers from deep.
bright sounds and dark sounds—soft insides
     from window on Greenpoint Ave
     offered coffee or fresh samanthas
     on a stomach curdled up
     & teeth raw from a strange sharp toothbrush
I was clean everywhere, homeless
(my wallet was clean, if not for the card that says I'm (still) me.)

    That morning I thought I'd just walk and walk, (and passing
      my house decided to pace it off indoors—)
    But the day old beer or the fear of adding to it gave me
      courage to polish my injury and set off, bikeless, to capture
      somehow the end of it. My last Greenpoint like my last West
      Tisbury and last Germantown
Like going to sleep.

What will numb it tonight if beer won't?
I had moved my empty room in boxes
My portrait of Marx was quite cold when I talked to him about it.
My Satchmo gone, playing only the itchy ends of the side (is this
    LIVE?).
The shadows bend towards late, crease and darken more.

The town appeared after the fog and disappeared again as the clouds
        came in and
disappears now at night,
save some yellow lights
faint like   candles on someone's porch.

I wait for fall, after the rain goes,
no more green paint or blue paint to buy
But brown and red and
a new axe to split the newfallen tree   to burn with me, late.

Roma Città Aborta

When they created the normal spell
The nubs of our hands burnished it
And were found old after

The wintering   recedes.

I'm back from the long arc, the bricklayer
Drug back from the city all its
Sexy Dumps—age-old crap, ancient
Dreamy city stuff
      A cardiac-smoke-pump
dancing and running its knees down me
I beg it to return—
(I was too young when they outlawed that.)

At night, in the fort, I twitch (snore?)
daily stagger under the rim
of farmers shade.
In the spring everything will be decided
the hulls of stripped ships , birch bark chips
who missed the landward star
banked heavy with the tide
all the lights suddenly blinking

We stole work on the path
our people pursued by stalkers
who own the road
the sad river sides
someone's dog is tied by their rope.

I Dreamed I Was a Boat

Morning Glory, your dirty hands,
      your long back & brown back & back that bends,
I would like to
          once again

in a field of flowers.

We are above the whole city
my mouth near the red petals
and all they surround

Just touched.

You press down & I think
    If you partake of the flesh, you become one

only taking is taking   away.
The summer is long, I am thirsty
growing only smaller
among these Missouri poppies.

The city's a wall
the river is deep
on the shores of Acheron
I've just crossed

On the beach of balanced stones
we are quiet
& watch the waves-that-no-boat-made

I see
through you   an inlet
to the sea.

Curt Circuit   *a shortcut.*

Upstairs, where the stains were, the marks of thy
Motion
All the sides of the coins said
"Tails,   You lose"

When on lonely rooftops, on Wightman avoiding
Civic responsibility: traffic claims court and my voting rights, an
"obstruction" never reconciled by community service
harmonizing above
the first spring day,
when the girl in the rainbow scarf said
hi.
when the soup kitchens and hunger strikes seemed so…

Down on when dawn expired
    we had a song about that
       all the voices echo, this is 1992, when
         I wished I'd never had a Volkswagon
until 1997, when dispersed overseas
I had The Great Old Swamp remastered
And the van sold.

     The night bike-battles through Schenley Park, the Carnegie
       melons
     Kiss parties (somehow a dawn in the cemetery) and
One West Virginia halloween
    One   disguised as drunken campers

One night walking home from grilling Allen Ginsberg's salmon
With an hour's-work-worth of beer, in the twenty below
I lost the heel of my boot.

Two Love Songs   X.00

I.

Oh, youngsides
Because maybe you have
nothing else

I don't want to touch anything
first.

II.

When you go away
I'll think about the colors (soft you)
against
My work,
Your shirt.

Prima Colazione

A garish dish and its garnish
Wet downstairs where William was

Una ballerina seduta

Landscape   *an epitaph*

Soon I'll be captured,
The lions anymore don't help.
There, my crib.

Separate dust, the stalks the sun rusted
Among branches, here I am.

Canti Isolani

Il Parassita Pasquale   *Canzone Pontina*

The window and all ebbs in
The sound of the coming   season

Slow motion from the banks of Frontone

     A glimmer from the port, the foghorn
     I hear   much later.
The bay at *all* hours reflects, I noted
     Spurting fish and wine among the artichokes
     The snakes and I startling each other
     and carrying on (and other things in the brush),
     the ginestra a sleepy spring against the wind
     and skeletons of giant cactus still as Roman statues—

& the sea always deep ultramarine   + light puddles / cerulean
     shadows
     slide projector of a sky
that altered intensity   at my every gag
and made a white spooky morning
to sleep through

Salt   *Cantu Siculu I*

I'm preserved
By the rock sea &
Its rest   when returning upwards
Left Quartz duggets & yellow silt

The hot tires help me   verbally, home
Straight past the upright and left at the leaning yucca,
Past the rotted pumpkins and a poem: "Him for Her. My Life."

Our skin   Dust on it   gets flavored

          (& what the sun   to us fish   does)

Capo Passero *Cantu Siculu II*

Her Barren Fort, lamped by Noon
Solid ochre and half   mirage

The barracks of a gutted cross, rigid and salt-shaved
Up between the straits of low palms and the edgy black beach

Her long entrance
Her heart a passage from sky   to earth   to sea,
a grave and
a well
a Saltwater Lòpez, Capt., there buried

Where we Swum, possessions on a raft
To the land of the abandoned:
     My Seaman's anchor
Her flaking red bones
Defensive arms,   reclining tilt,   still
in the sharp grass
the bodies of boats were stripped   and piled on with bundles of nets
guarded by a padlock and a sooty pig.

Oiled in the current, straight to the shoals, banks and pockets
barely, with my toes
homed it
long body, savage rag, zoom lens and all
traced ourselves further down the map.

—What thirst, the hotwater
In our nakedness we saw nothing else.

La Tenda   *Cantu Siculu III*

In all that steam
Sweaty half-napped raft ride
Or on straw and *bastardi*

All our folds we'd emptied of sand
Rinsed our tan suits
Fortified with oil

With you, My High Seas
     So much floating   in the muggy afternoon

        In our little oven.

A Hallucination and a Flashback
Cantu Siculu IV

>*O Sun, in your lonesomeness*
>*What you do*

Favored for her legs, the saddest Darkness
By the Fish Fires and the Reggae, or
Drying her hair in a honeycomb of mirrors
Burnt like an adolescent
By that boundary.

From above my cards, an ace of Spades, I saw

the weekend ping-pong matches
Possibility and   Loss and then   "There's always next summer"
To stay

waiting to cross paths
Or glare by the sinks,
        cleaning the Squid and Capone
        Against the windy red sunset.

SchoolGirlSongs

'a marea

I heard the sandsacks have boiled again from the ridges and bank—
Shot with a magic arm
Or just gone out with the tide
    & Back to Bed.

I heard the mountain's hot and closing the day
That faithful spat and the cavern emptied itself out.
It's all becoming clearer
The less I sleep.

Class First

"you're heavy with your black and aren't reading
It's all going quite well   ….good."   Even
beautiful

as soon as you breathe
til dawn
I walk behind.

who   told   you   to—
         w/ skeleton on your heels

from bus stop to shoulder
your long air   .

And, when bringing up nothing, I
Struck a (tender) chord =^★:

My bones won't forget

The pleasure they never had.

Fishers of Mang

Forlorn was
The new apostle, so unused to the fish and travel -
"shall I clear the dives or shovel?"
enough peace—
      for now
...
soaked in
a man-white-shirt
seeing his data zip flat
& the final bass turn to crash,
seeing the soldiers and the morgue—

what's in my ear
        on my lips
turned cold.

above the baptistry
"feathered" light

sing (& sniff) below God's part.

Natural Act

Lofty in the narrows, or
the motion of her back
Who knocked   that
Stuff on the floor
Who in text sent warning and
Pretext to
Natural walks or
"talking over drinks"
about our common records:
To let me climb her tree
& her mine

shifty, though, in the sweet summer
sheets and afterwards,
in LittleItaly.

from Philly, all fountains and flags,
the speckled roads lead out
the Indian river

from dense Home, the road leads in.

River Song I   *a pre-river song.*

The sizzling comets
under the dream-catcher-wind-chimes
push us closer
in your hair

masks glare back and wooden boxes chatter
there and then

I try not to move

& smoke from your pack.

River Song II   Sul Tevere.

I left (leapt) too abruptly,
talked too much & spelled out
the line of the mountains   more
than you

Against the backcrop of river, of
Age and haze, sticks and tall-bank-grass,
A stretch made lunar by tractor—
I noticed
every gesture, curve, color, your
Two flat teeth
your brushes
between the scarecrows and
your guardian angel

River Song III

You're the dawn's cooter
Twilight in the high-zone
     with your morning mist,
     the river's swell and curve,
     and a memory about the eyes-of-your-lines.
Those hands as you splattered, distracted, colored

the new me & the new you.

You're surrounded now   by the valley
The river is a bottle inside
     sleeping where hands touch
     In the fresh season
By the body longing beside us,   towards Rome.

You're the sweet upwards   where the stars are
When they are, or   What the mountains, too, aim towards:
The hand of the cloud
Black or white, over the blue.

You're the sand/which I packed; my brown bag, my juke box

not quite a love-affair.

The sideways side of a shoe horn

The lemon drops and all
Female buttons
Blanking the eyes
For the brain to
Hurt on
And wake up shifting in the night.

Skimming with Hosts

Two days into spring, in the year 2001
I will have swam
Through the sharks and the glass
And cool currents and jellyfish-tankers
On a stolen sailboat with a crew of me
To a Beach Near You
      With a can in my pocket
      to protect me from the bullets
and
with something else in mind.

Exploring the ships and posing
above Plymouthrock for a photo that doesn't exist
I depart (Back   across .

SOS   *a reoccurring dream, NY to RM*

Across these
Cold hands, cold mind
Sweet perplexed between phone calls &
Messages

Our lonesome broadcast
Spell out

You can't be kept there
Or here

Straniero

About as far from Shadyside as
Friendship,
and just about as far West as East
From here
        much water under an invisible bridge
        in the cloudy night

        & my (warm) skin
        in the river.

There were fireworks tonight
Some San Antonio brightened behind the back
Of the black pines

Moving under the moon to feast.

The Archaeologist

this
that hasn't in Cuba closed or Egypt begun

an October in your City.

I miss the
fleshy
present

Between Pilgrim's Progress
& Plymouth Rock
In
space
Without
history or physic
s
&
w/out   Map.

The song of shlongs   *un sogno*

      the witches broom and wing of
that   and
then the sand
and hand-bandages, esp. the Fingertips,
from the Lime and the Glue

holes fold the dry cavern
blood's pitted against the sand
hauled from my
back again

the famous eyebags frame—

are you sure the weeds won't film me
when I hide?

The Two Februaries

I am up this morning
Breaking sticks in the dark for a fire
To warm my water

The wind blanches all sounds,
The light will make us bats.

One kills what the other calls:
Daffodils bulbed and the dawn lifting

Still   no sound   of dogs barking
Just the night through the wood   calling
The cats bristly weight
Between our nightbreath

To which side I finally strained
in this dream.

Birthday Suites

Plot

Under the growth
the stunted pilot, the army
grows
under the cot.

The log, neck-long, from the fire
Spits
Like a dozen soft shells.

Are you ready for the disaster?

I'm in charge
With a headline
From all this rain.

A Nation of Williams

Of it the Ravenspoke:
Who stole our sugar through the painted brown paper
With magic burnt my brother's eyebrows and legs
Eyes back, in his own inferno

the cool rushes back
after
whatever we forget.

Hudson Lark

The dump-metal horse
and my landscape, across the side
from bank, outwards from backlit
stood still

I'm shooting.

The house has lips
coral
& sides   my hands hold down—
whatever you're sure of   we'll make due with

or is it the end of my hand
cut neatly off
left   after the blood-faucet
in this heaping bandage

the pine-for-miles.

I's sorry the words th't drove off the wintr bit hardr dis spring

& the marsh that we filled
while trying to gain ground

(our glorified bridge: mountain onward)

Even the gridded city glows
like typed cotton paper

like water   in an earthquake
circles

like the bricks stacked against us.

Dream   *reoccurring, II*

In the half empty house of corridors
an invisible boar skull followed me.
the bedrooms and bathrooms connect, an attic is my cellar, basements
        our roofs,
the kitchen   mostly empty
just stacked with   plates

Is da Sasquatch coming to kill me
as I
stick in
the deep
snow?

Is my arm asleep?

Interior

Pitted against the real-sides' softly coming
our nourishment by the bathwater in the bake-light
the saddle soap is by my cream, the tile is cool
on my back with the brush
only this snoring

your friends left the water on
brought Port, asked for seconds then
for the draft, the small porch, and the char
Who was it hollering through the basement?

If I just had socks on this floor and
took off

light slats tilt down, the sun were under.

The Fish Are Still

I'm coerced by the Stewardess
us two silent engines in the night
and the cold sea outside—

I call Cognac.

Under Sentimental Music and the American's barn-talk
the dark to the North expires—
the dawn
     stirs

I Buckle-up and beckon
her hallway shuffle
nipples as witness—
& write another poem called "How Bad is Heathrow"

and order one more.

My letter says
"Let's resolve,"
and
I watch the flight.

One of the Last Poems of July

Through Jesi, the stacked trucks
like the rubble, here coming &
      the rubber bottles we ran over.
at Sushi Bar in Portonovo, in a cove
the blind keep playing their song
by the tide
she keeps taking my money, touching my hand
we keep saying we'll go   but never do

all that wine I'd never had   made me love her.

The last night we stayed up &
before boarding for sunrise opened another Sangrantino
John came from his hammock, complimented the blanket, cursed the
      dogs
the Frenchman came in his Hawaiian shirt, shitty & reeking like the
      night, hours before

I in my hemlock
& you in your Japanese coma, calm but not yet gone

It was a sad march, blind
against the tide   going.

The Last Poem of July

the dawn fogged-up and lifted

Light hissed
through, then
blue shadows
made   the hills—

we'll have emptied the maze
now let's, in the heat   be black & blue by morning.

give me another vowel

the world has balls   to Fail
me: a   pointed fly
         equidistant from a dead yellow rose, a potholder,
         an ashtray and a glass of water-now-gone
flies away

so bitter is the gum that chews me.

October

The curtains' unblindfold
wherewithin from haveyoucome   thru all the yellowlight

as I heaved some   with a fork   weeds
thismorning is sketched on my skin   this song

this series of scars we will have achieved

outnumbered by flies   as I heard somewhere said

on the veil between interior

★   ★   ★

I try to go on: empty the lawn of its habits

the face of my coin faints after reflecting
as I scratch sweating the surface
to bury a brown bag full
and to find out
what's under
the dirt.

★   ★   ★

Now we're washed up
with the wind closing the snow around
makes you wonder
the blue of your scarf in the black and white and the grey

the capitol of the cross winds

I'm sure we're up to no good—*how are you feeling?*

It's hard to swallow the bird in this Bush
It's hard to swallow the little monkey with banana

Or, I just miss my bike, and climbing down
the empty graves of Point Breeze.

Cod of Signs

1.
Lost in the spell of devilmoss: I am animal,
stuffed in the car like a metal weasel who sheds
his light on
you
who picked from those branches
you,
and put yourself under oil.

take this shallow leap and leave me out of it
or swallow.

2.
you're heavy salted
split open for toasting
against the small weeds and against the tall weeds
Towards the sea-of-no-islands
Wishing
back and forth as the moon tugs at you
or us
who've since   determination   lost

3.
he is splendid, you're alluring
be careful where you cast your hair
light makes us invisible
water, transparent.

Two Ships, an Ocean Liner, a Buoy, and a Seagirl

Passing through me / you *are* what you say, right?

In the shaken sea held still, or
on the arc of the tidal wave that'd wreck us
I simmer
& Moses it open, the sea and the entire continent

you are west and equally east and I have never seen you

full, content / just boy and gull.

The Blue on Rot   *an epitaph*

Glass capillaries, Blue in the
air-clear flesh
Grow on my old Bones, here lain.

Branches in the Stone Soup.

The SomeHighway Poems

A Late Bday Wish

jeez, this haze
slowly the trees brush
Luna pants and ignores the lizards
& the deafening crickets.
Umbria is dust and it's only May
Late, after all the rain
The elms push again and sway to stop
Featherly pend and settle their compass

The heat makes dark.

We are only arms now, from shoulder down
As long as the valley we reach over
to comb the mountaintop of its fleas
& the scratched undersides that I made this morning
against this briar
Under this sun, before lunch.

Somedays I'm not up for the challenge

Usually at six with Mambo Kids chips and chickencoop wine
The mountain seems an ass
The insects feed on me starting now and
a constellation of rhombus and oblong ellipse
shapes rise up on veiny ankles and knuckles
I start another crossword puzzle (& leave another incomplete).

This, after many non-committal walks, much flipping the tape and lunch
And some half-hearted dabbing into the cerulean sky
of another unfinished painting.

Ferro di Cavallo

Where circling in the evening, lost
I'd left the Q8,
the long dirt road, the house with car, the dog,
those drawings, the seeds
she grew
the table about to collapse, the herbs
she leaned over
her Spanish, her beer, her back   arched
her broken toe, dirty sock, ankle, leg, hip
as she tripped over the group of dogs
near the mossy pool
And almost (as if) her tears
At least a stutter
fear and (I, too, catch my breath)
What we wanted to

Soft eye, cheek, hair
All near

Still Life with Live Model

Made of months
In many positions
both aware and at rest
reclined reflects my
stare
without thinking
just the passage, her
feathery fingers pass my ear.
I risk touching only
the gauze of her toe
her wrist where bracelet is
the edge of the bottle where she sipped,
& watch
the back of her wander off to water the plants
fuss in the kitchen
& disappear

of thick lines and delicate invisible lines
all her limbs are joined.

The First Poem of July

Everything is still and white-washed
the cicada seem so far, and so many
This is all I wanted to do anyway
Just not alone.
There's no working on my clouds today
No contrast and no soft shapes to pile the paint for, no yellow light
just a sparrow and the thunder
that sounds like a plane over the sea, about as far off as the cicada.

That's not like my body, to lean over and weep
a leafy shift in the heat
that it doesn't know what to do with.

My North, Your South

Listening to the void I heard you were well
That you'd returned
& through all those miles (to think) to think that you'd call—

tonight
we're in the mountains-between-us
like last night   your voice
it   is   still

one of us had better go

I can proceed North or retreat to from-where-the-clouds-come
(there they are, with a storm)
or you can come South with me
at least halfway
just to where the mountain is.

I'm sure
Tomorrow
you'll decide.

D-76

Once in the dark we burnt black the clouds
& left some white, stood
so close we nearly fell.
Then yesterday the traffic slowed and
we got off
to have a cold drink near the quarry

& no one said a word.

Poem on a Cold September Evening
newspaper & death ravioli

Smoke low in the valley
inches before first light
so blues
the distance:
A piece of skypaper on the embers
that the ash evening ends.

One dead chicken and three giant Chinese chickens on my hands
One egg & a half dozen rusty nuts and washers
A branch fire to burn

Tonight I'll have to go get it & throw it
in the dumpster.

A Day at the Races

Now that the compass works & the axel turns & the tires finally tread
I'm off north over the rocks
To the pits that broke both axel and compass
& the ordinary confusion
& what they call "sin."
There was a passenger. Not the beer sweating between my legs
Nor Future City Radio nor David Allen Coe.
There's no dog in the rearview
The cigarette is already doing its job
like the road holding me up
& the clouds who observe
& transform
like a passenger that rides, compliments the car
holds on for dear life
kisses you goodbye

Good Thing You're Not Here to Listen to the Nothing

The morning just gets darker, wilts under
the heavy shade of clouds
at rest on the mountain
so even the smoke stays low and grave.

I was about to send a sign, some longing, just to deepen the line
the awkward space
      I see the side of you (who never looks   directly)
through
and more comfortable in breadth.

Better to wish than to regret.

Only the gold fields differ
And a dark blue cloud in the grey sky
Where the mountain rocks back.

Whiter Still

Hills appear & vanish
Through the linen & silky clouds
Valleys sink, pressed by shadow
In your landscape.
Lay on this table
Show the trees and gullies.

First covered with snow   that melts to touch
Feathers shedding & anything left
Torn (like lace).
Then the spring mud
Some hair & some spit
A thousand kisses
the light rain that stops.
Then the shifting sky, some reddish
sweating   at this empty hour.
The tree snuggles with the fox
The seasons change
It's hot, but snows anyway
Over these olive trees, again.

ABOUT THE AUTHOR

William Pettit is a painter and poet. His poetry has been published in *To:*, *Phoebe*, and *POM*. His paintings have been shown in Philadelphia, Rome, and Paris. Pettit lives with his wife and two children in the countryside near Rome. He teaches art at the John Cabot University in Rome, and at the Umbra Institute in Perugia, Italy.

ABOUT THESE POEMS

These are landscape poems, poems of seasons. And they are love songs. The Landscape is of observation and experience. Love is of loss and recollection.
There are home poems, road poems, boat poems, the locus is circumscribed. Until love and loss crumble them.

They are songs of failure. Language fails and Romance fails. Faith fails. So they are at times absurd poems: reduced to stuttering acceptance. They are letters and they are confessions.
They are songs to the vanished, written from across the cold ocean.

wp

www.ingramcontent.com/pod-product-compliance
Lightning Source LLC
Chambersburg PA
CBHW051707040426
42446CB00008B/766